On the Job™

with an

ARCHITECT
BUILDER OF THE WORLD

Jake Miller
Illustrated by Susan Gal

BARRON'S

First edition for the United States and Canada published
exclusively by Barron's Educational Series, Inc. in 2001

Copyright © 2001 by Orange Avenue Publishing, Inc.
Created and produced by Orange Avenue Publishing, Inc., San Francisco
Illustrations © 2001 by Susan Gal

All inquiries should be addressed to:
Barron's Educational Series, Inc.
250 Wireless Boulevard
Hauppauge, NY 11788
http://www.barronseduc.com

Library of Congress Catalog Card No. 2001135076

International Standard Book No. 0-7641-1867-6

Printed in Singapore
9 8 7 6 5 4 3 2 1

ARCHITECT
BUILDER OF THE WORLD

Meet Bridgit and Hugo.

They are friends and neighbors. Together they guide readers through the exciting world of various careers.

In *On the Job with an Architect,* Bridgit and Hugo meet Miguel and Julia, two architects who are designing a sunporch for Hugo's neighbor, Mrs. Oscar. Bridgit and Hugo visit Miguel and Julia at their office and learn the nitty-gritty of what it takes to be an architect.

Table of Contents

CHAPTER 1
Bridgit and Hugo Build a Fort 6

CHAPTER 2
What Architecture Is 10

CHAPTER 3
What Architects Do.......16

CHAPTER 4 Job Training..............28

CHAPTER 5 Saying Good-Bye.............30

Activities........................32

Glossary.........................46

Resources.......................47

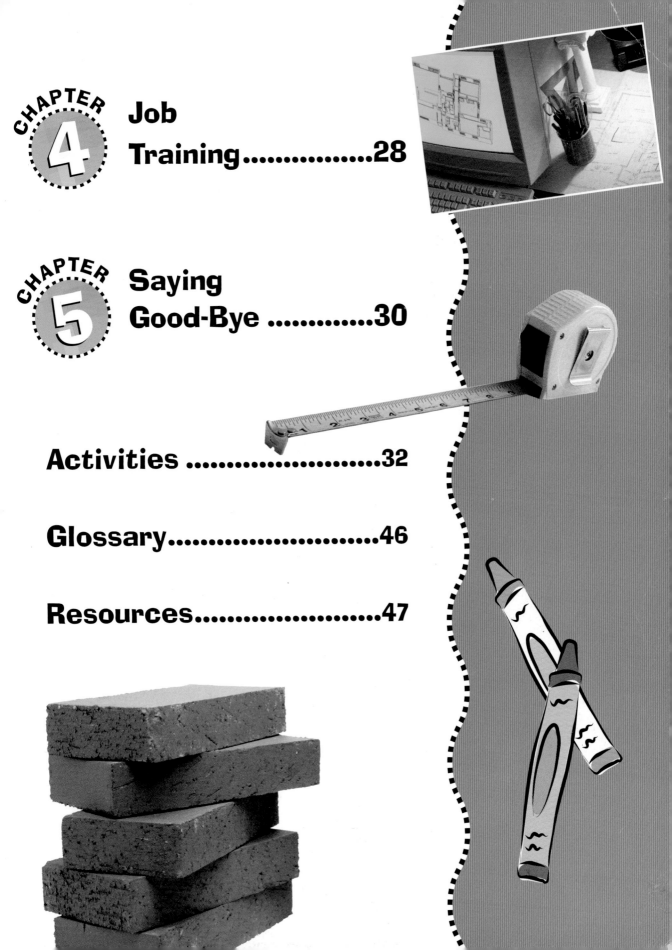

CHAPTER 1

Bridgit and Hugo Build a Fort

Hugo and Bridgit are building a fort in the backyard.

"This fort is going to be awesome, Bridgit, but I can't decide if it should be four or five stories tall. It sure would be fun to have a lookout platform on the top, so we could see all the way over to the playground," Hugo says.

I'll just borrow this one little piece...

"That would be cool, Hugo, but I'm not sure we have enough wood here to make it that tall. And I'm worried about what would happen if we were up there in a heavy wind," Bridgit says.

Just then, Mrs. Oscar, Hugo's next-door neighbor, comes over to the fence to say hello. Alongside are a man and a woman whom Bridgit and Hugo don't know.

"Looks like you kids are having some of the same fun we are," says Mrs. Oscar. "I want to add a sunporch to the back of my house, so I hired Miguel and Julia to help me. They're architects."

"We just came over to take a look at the house and the neighborhood, so we could figure out how to get started with our design," says Julia.

"We like to have an idea of what the site looks like before we start sketching or building models," says Miguel. "I think I have a great idea for a Victorian-style greenhouse, with lots of glass and steel."

"In the beginning, I like to think more about the kinds of shapes that might go into the finished project: triangles, rectangles, and curves," Julia says.

CHAPTER 2

What Architecture Is

"That sounds more like building a fort than a real grown-up's job," Bridgit says. "Do you really get to sit around all day and play with blocks and imagine beautiful buildings?"

"Well, daydreaming and designing are only part of what we do. Our clients wouldn't be too happy if we spent all of our time coming up with fancy, fantastic ideas," Julia says. "The important thing is figuring out what kinds of buildings or projects our clients need, and then finding a way to get them built."

11

"One of our most important jobs is communication. We need to be able to listen to our clients so we can understand their needs. When we come up with designs we like, we have to be able to show our clients the interesting design possibilities. That's where the sketches and models come in," Miguel says.

Julia adds, "Architects have to be generalists—that means we need to know enough about a lot of different things, so that we can talk to other experts and understand what they're telling us."

I was hoping for something a little BIGGER...

INFO STRUCTURE

After an architect designs a building, it takes a whole team of experts working together to build it.

Engineers contribute with their technical knowledge of materials, structures, and systems. They do the math to ensure that the architectural design will be strong and safe.

Fire and **building inspectors** make sure that the project follows important rules. They determine things such as the number and size of fire exits and sprinkler systems, and the safe use of materials.

Contractors bring hands-on experience in the techniques of constructing a building. Some contractors specialize in one area—**plumbing, bricklaying,** or **carpentry**—while **general contractors** coordinate the work of all the specialists, according to the architect's specifications. For example, the general contractor makes sure that the walls are built before the painters show up on the job site.

Landscape architects specialize in designing the lawns, gardens, and other plantings that surround a building.

13

Miguel points out, "Architecture isn't just about designing buildings and adding on back porches, either. Architects can help plan an entire brand-new city, revitalize a run-down neighborhood, and find new transportation solutions. They can build a mall or an office complex, design a skyscraper, or create a single beautiful, comfortable, sunny window seat."

"Architecture is all about designing places
that work: places that inspire you to worship, museums that let
you think about art, a train station that makes it easy and exciting
to come into a big city, or a park that helps you
relax once you
get there,"
Julia says.

CHAPTER 3
What Architects Do

"Wow, that sounds like a complicated job. How do you go about it?" Bridgit asks.

"We just break it down and do it one step at a time. Why don't you hang out with us for a while and see how we do it?" Miguel asks. "We can start right here, with Mrs. Oscar's sunporch."

"Super!" Hugo says.

"The first step is scoping out the job," Julia says. "That means we look at the site, talk with our client, and figure out the detailed requirements of the project."

"What we design must both look good and work well, inside and outside, and it can't cost more than the client can afford to pay."

"I've always wanted a Victorian-style porch," says Mrs. Oscar, "but I want to see what Julia and Miguel think will work best for this house. Then I'll make a decision!"

"So design isn't only about looks, it's also about how it all fits together," Hugo says.

"That's right, Hugo. And that means we have to start thinking about all the different factors that might affect the building," Julia says. "What will the building look like at different times of the day or during different seasons of the year? Where will the light fall? Which way does the wind blow? What happens to all the water when it rains?"

"Besides natural forces, we have to consider human-made things like traffic noise or the other kinds of buildings there are in the neighborhood."

Julia and Miguel take the kids back to their office to see the next phase of the project.

"We spend a lot of time on the design phase. Sometimes one of us will work on a project alone, or sometimes we'll both tackle it together. It's great to have a partner to bounce ideas off of," Julia says. "Sometimes the ideas change shape over and over before we get it right."

"After we agree with our client on the basic design of a project, we start working on the computer. We use software made for engineers and architects that helps us draw accurately and quickly. For every project, we need to make lots and lots of careful drawings of all the parts and pieces with different views and different scales," Miguel says. "We show and describe what they are and how they fit together."

Can mine have a Jacuzzi?

PLAN

ELEVATION

SECTION

SCALE

A **plan** is a view of a building from straight above, so you can see how a floor will be laid out.

An **elevation** is a view of how the front, sides, or back of a building will look.

A **section** is like an elevation, only it's a slice of the inside of a building—which you could never see in real life—that lets you see what the structures inside the walls will look like.

Architects use different **scales** to share different kinds of information: a close-up of an important design detail or a broad view of how a building fits into the landscape around it.

21

"These drawings go all the way from a scribble on a scrap of paper to the detailed drawings and blueprints that tell you, brick by brick and with every water faucet, electrical outlet, and door knob accounted for, just how a building should be built," Julia explains.

"We have to make sure our plans are safe, and that they meet all the legal requirements for building in the neighborhood where the project will stand," Miguel says.

Architects have to talk to scientists, civil engineers, electrical engineers, mechanical engineers, structural engineers, technicians, and lawyers, who specialize in the different aspects of building construction.

"We have to know how the materials we have chosen will stand up to different forces, whether the building is strong enough for hurricanes and earthquakes, and if there are enough fire exits and other safety features," Miguel says.

"Sounds complicated," Hugo says.

"Well, some architects like to think about design, and some like to think about ways to make all the different systems work together. It's like a big puzzle," Miguel says.

"It can be fun to try to juggle all these different aspects of the project," Julia says. "You always have to learn new things, and you have to make sure all your partners in the project know what they need to do."

Miguel adds, "Once the plans are all made and the details are worked out, the architects assist the client in choosing a contractor who actually builds the project. We visit the construction site often to inspect the work, answer questions, and make sure the project is being built correctly with the intended materials and equipment."

"Wow, architects are really the organizers that make it all come together," Hugo says.

"That's a good way of thinking about it," Miguel says. "We're not just designing the structure of the building, we're helping people structure their lives."

"A building isn't just concrete and glass. It's a space that people live and work in. When you put a group of buildings together, you get a neighborhood. When people make decisions about how to build their neighborhoods, they're really making decisions about how they want to live with one another," Julia says.

"Wow, when you think about how long a building can last, those are really important decisions," Bridgit says.

Job Training

"So how do you get ready for such a big responsibility?" Hugo asks.

"Well, it's a combination of education and experience. First you have to get a special college degree in architecture. That can take anywhere from five to eight years of study," Julia says.

"That has to cover a lot of ground: art, history, engineering, science, writing, drawing . . . ," Miguel adds.

"Once you get your degree, you have to do an internship with a licensed architect, so that you can learn how the job is done in the real world. Professors and clients can have very different ways of grading your success," Julia says.

"After you've completed your internship, you must take a test to get your license, covering the different things you've learned. That's one more way to make sure that every building will be built safely."

Many different materials can be used to make a building. Simple walls of compacted soil are used in everything from one-room huts to giant hydroelectric dams. The ancients learned to harness the strength of stone and brick arches to support tall buildings. Today's architects are constantly exploring new building techniques, using everything from high-tech metals to recycled paper in their designs.

5 Saying Good-Bye

Miguel and Julia and the kids return to Hugo's backyard, where the sketches, blocks, and raw materials for the fort are still piled.

"Architecture sounds like a lot of work, but if you put your mind to it, you can do it. There's no reason why you can't get started right now," Julia says.

"Good luck with your fort
—and have fun,"
Miguel says.

Activities

Being an architect is a creative, challenging job that requires a special set of abilities. You might be surprised at how many of the most important skills you already have.

- Do you like to draw, and to think about shapes and light and textures?

- Do you like to see how pieces fit together to make a whole?

- Do you like to understand why things work the way they do?

Try the following activities on your own, or with a group of friends, and find out if you have what it takes to be an architect!

1 Draw Your Dream House........34

2 Design 36

3 Favorite Places 37

4 Make a Bad Place Better 38

5 Light Show 39

6 Water, Water, Everywhere....40

7 Materials Matter....................42

8 Texture Fun..........................43

9 Build a Fort...........................44

ACTIVITY 1

Draw Your Dream House

Architects use all kinds of different drawings—with different scales and views from different angles —to give a sense of what the whole project will look like when it's done.

Imagine you could live in any kind of house you want, anywhere in the world. Where would your house be, and what would it look like?

Is it on a beach, in a mountain valley, or nestled in the topmost branches of a tall tree?

What would your favorite neighborhood look like?

• Draw your dream house, showing what the whole building will look like.

• Draw different views—from the front, back, side, top, and bottom. Remember that not all parts of the house are visible from one spot. For example, the secret submarine exit underneath the house would be invisible from above, because it is covered by the pony stables and the roller coaster.

- Draw smaller details of the house. Does your beach house have a wave pattern carved in the wood of the front door? Is your secret cave inlaid with diamonds? Do you have an indoor garden?

When you sketch, don't worry about making mistakes. Draw quickly, let the ideas flow, and use your pencil more than your eraser. In the end, you may find that what you like best is something you drew by accident.

Design

Some architects like to show three different versions of every project to their clients, so they can see the different ways to reach their goals.

Make a series of sketches for a playground you'd like to build.

- Start with a quick sketch, then refine the drawing and add more details.

- Make sure you show how it will fit into the neighborhood and add close-ups of important details.

ACTIVITY 3

Favorite Places

Use all five senses (seeing, hearing, smelling, touching, and tasting) to help you describe your favorite place.

- How does it make you feel when you are there?

- How do you use the space?

- Have you made any changes to the space to make it even better?

Also, think about how the space feels at different times of the day and during different seasons.

ACTIVITY 4

Make a Bad Place Better

Think about a place that makes you feel uncomfortable or that just seems unpleasant.

- Describe it with all five senses in mind.

- Think of things you could do to make this place better.

Whew! Air freshener would be good...

Light Show

Light is one of the most important factors in defining how a building feels.

Shiny metal buildings glisten in the sun. Big windows and skylights make the rooms bright and warm.

Make a scrapbook:

- Clip pictures from magazines that show interesting shadows, lighting, and reflections.

- Add sketches or pictures you have taken of your house or neighborhood.

- Make a sketch of your favorite spot in the house at different times of the day. Where is the light coming from?

Water, Water, Everywhere

The next time it rains, put on your raincoat, get out your umbrella, and head out into the great, wet world outside your door.

Walk around your house and around your block. Count how many different places you see water flowing.

- Does it run down the windows?

- Does it drip off the edge of the roof, or does it collect in gutters and pour out a spout?

- Are there any puddles or tiny ponds that collect the water before it can flow away?

- Does all the water flow away, or is some of it stored somewhere to be used later?

**Imagine you are a
raindrop, and trace your path
from the sky to the storm drains.**

- What happens if you fall on the roof?

- What if you fall on the lawn?

- What if you fall on the sidewalk?

What if you fall
on the dog?

It's important for architects to think about water: how to get water into a building for everyone to drink; how to get water and the waste it carries to flow out of a building; and how to make sure the roof doesn't leak and let water in to weaken the building's structure.

ACTIVITY 7

Materials Matter

To see how different kinds of material can be used to build different kinds of structures, try to build a model home using only:

- Playing cards

- Folded construction paper with no tape

- Modeling clay

- Construction paper and tape with no folds

- Sand

- Gravel

- Mud bricks dried in the sun

- Styrofoam trays and toothpicks

ACTIVITY 8

Texture Fun

Take a crayon and some newsprint or drawing paper with you on a walk.

• Put the paper against an interesting texture, and gently rub the side of the crayon on the paper.

• Make a note of how each texture feels to the touch and how it looks in the light.

Build a Fort

Now's your chance to be the architect of your own building, from start to finish. Your fort can be as simple as a blanket draped on the couch in the living room on a rainy day, or as complicated as a tree house with trapdoors and a rope ladder.

Find a location that suits your needs. Think about how your structure will fit into the neighborhood. Do you want it to blend in for secrecy or stand out to make a statement?

Sketch your fort. Try different designs before you settle on the one you like best. Keep in mind the materials you have to work with and try to be realistic, but don't let that stop your imagination from running a little bit wild.

Include the features that will suit your purposes, like lots of look-out holes for bird-watching—and people-watching, too.

Show the sketches to an adult and get permission to build. (That's like meeting with the building inspector.) Once your plans are completed and permitted, start building.

Don't forget to get help from the experts, just like a real architect. Have an adult drive you to the lumberyard, and help you with the carpentry. If you're using blankets and tarps to make a tent-fort, you may not need much help. If you're doing woodworking and bricklaying, you probably will. Remember: Make sure the building is safe.

Glossary

Code   A set of rules or laws governing certain aspects of a project. Fire codes deal with safety in case of fire, and other codes regulate systems like the electrical and waste removal systems in a building.

Elevation   A view of what the front, side, or back of a building will look like.

Engineering   The science of using structures and materials safely and efficiently.

Materials   All the stuff a building is made out of.

Plan   A view from straight above, so you can see how a horizontal surface, like a floor or an entire building site, will be laid out.

Program   The architect's vision for how the project will be designed, developed, built, and used, as agreed to by the client.

Scale   The relative size of a drawing to the object it represents. A small scale lets an architect draw a whole building on one piece of paper to get an overall sense of the space. A large scale lets an architect show how particular details of the building will look.

Section   A drawing that shows the structures that will not be seen in the finished product, such as what is inside a wall, floor, or roof.

Structure   The arrangement of parts that make up a whole; the way pieces of a building fit together to do a particular job.

Resources

Careers in Architecture
Careers in Architecture Program
The American Institute of
 Architects
1735 New York Avenue NW
Washington, DC 20006

Famous Architects
Sandra Jordan & Jan Greenburg
Frank O. Gehry, Outside In
New York: DK Publishing, 2000

Kathleen Thorne-Thomsen
Frank Lloyd Wright for Kids
Chicago: Chicago Review Press,
 1994

Ginger Wadsworth
Julia Morgan, Architect of Dreams
Minneapolis: Lerner Publications,
 1990

How Architecture Works
Michael J. Crosbie
*Arches to Zigzags: An Architecture
 ABC*
New York: Harry N. Abrams,
 2000

J. E. Gordon
*Structures: Or, Why Things Don't
 Fall Down*
Cambridge, Mass.: Da Capo
 Press, 1988

Saralinda Hooker
*The Art of Construction: Project
 and Principles for Beginning
 Engineers and Architects*
Chicago: Chicago Review Press,
 1990

David Macaulay
Building Big
Castle
Cathedral
City
Boston: Houghton Mifflin, 2000,
 1981, 1982, 1983

Drawing
Quentin Blake
*Drawing for the Artistically
 Undiscovered*
Palo Alto, Calif.: Klutz Press,
 1999

The books in this series are produced by Orange Avenue, Inc.
Creative Director: Hallie Warshaw
Writer: Jake Miller
Design & Production: Britt Menendez, B Designs
Illustrator: Susan Gal
Editor: Robyn Brode
Photographer: Britt Menendez, B Designs
Creative Assistant: Emily Vassos
Models: Emily Vassos, Holger Hugh Menendez

Consultants: Architects Timo Lindman, New York, and Brent Stringfellow, Boston; and Robin Ellerthorpe, director of facilities consulting at an architecture firm, Chicago

Special Thanks to: Amanda Smith Miller; Holger Hugh Menendez for the use of his architectural drawings; Connie Johnson for the use of her yard; and Ariel and Nina Krietzman for building the fort

Photo Credits: Artville, Corbis, Eyewire, John Foxx Images, Photodisc, Stockbyte, West Stock, and www.Comstock.com